AUSTON MATTHEWS

HOCKEY SUPERSTAR

BY RYAN WILLIAMSON

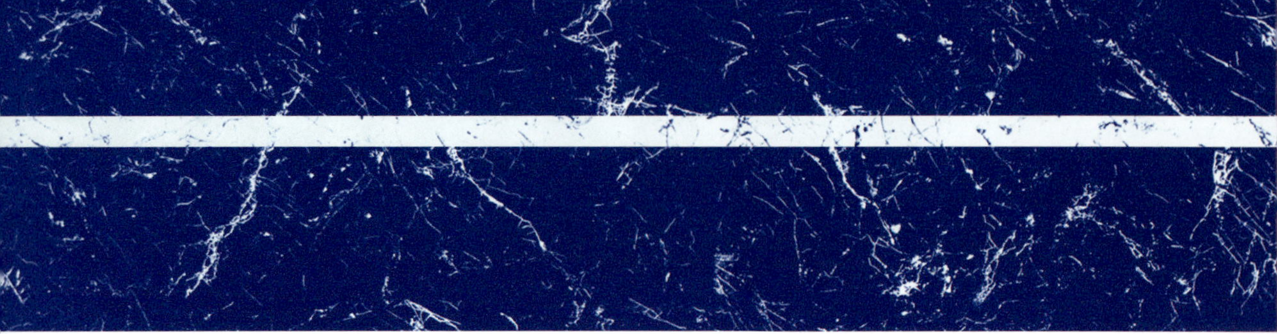

First Edition
First Printing, 2019

Book design by Jake Nordby
Cover design by Jake Nordby
Photographs ©: Keith Gillett/Icon Sportswire/AP Images, cover, 1, back cover; Steven Kingsman/Icon Sportswire, 4–5, 8, 10–11; Sean Kilpatrick/The Canadian Press/AP Images, 7; John Crouch/Icon Sportswire, 12, 18; Roni Rekomaa/Lehtikuva/AP Images, 15; Katerina Sulova/CTK/AP Images, 17; Gerry Angus/Icon Sportswire, 21, 23; Fred Kfoury III/Icon Sportswire, 24; Nathan Denette/The Canadian Press/AP Images, 27; Red Line Editorial, 29; John Crouch/AP Images, 30

Press Box Books, an imprint of Press Room Editions.

Library of Congress Control Number: 2019936730

ISBN
978-1-63494-102-0 (library bound)
978-1-63494-111-2 (paperback)
978-1-63494-120-4 (epub)
978-1-63494-129-7 (hosted ebook)

Distributed by North Star Editions, Inc.
2297 Waters Drive
Mendota Heights, MN 55120
www.northstareditions.com

Printed in the United States of America

About the Author

Ryan Williamson is a sportswriter based in the Minneapolis–Saint Paul area. His articles have appeared in various publications across the United States. He graduated from the University of Missouri with a degree in print/digital sports journalism. He lives with his miniature dachshund Minny.

TABLE OF CONTENTS

34
BAUER
TORONTO
MAPLE
LEAFS
34
NEXUS

1 A DEBUT FOR THE AGES

Auston Matthews skated into position in front of the goalie. From behind the net, a Toronto Maple Leafs teammate sent him a quick pass. When the puck arrived, Matthews poked it forward with a flick of his wrist. The puck flew past the diving Ottawa Senators goalie and into the net. Matthews pumped his fist as his teammates surrounded him in celebration.

Matthews had good reason to be excited. The rookie had just scored his first goal in the National Hockey League (NHL).

Matthews looks for an opportunity during a 2016 game against the Ottawa Senators.

It came just eight minutes into his first game. Toronto fans expected a lot out of Matthews. After all, he had been the No. 1 overall pick in the 2016 NHL Entry Draft. And his night was just getting started.

Later in the first period, Matthews had the puck on his stick once again. He bolted down the left side of the ice and fired a shot. The puck bounced off the goalie's leg and into the back of the net. Matthews had taken only two shots in the game so far. Both had resulted in goals.

Less than two minutes into the second period, Leafs defenseman Morgan Rielly streaked down the left boards. As Rielly brought the puck behind the net, Matthews skated into position in front of the goalie. Matthews received the pass and smacked a

Matthews (right) celebrates after scoring a goal in the first game of his career.

one-timer into the net. Even though the game was in Ottawa, hats rained down onto the ice. Matthews had just become the first No. 1 draft pick to score a hat trick in his first game.

Hats covered the ice after Matthews scored his third goal of the night.

Near the end of the second period, the score was tied 3–3. Toronto's William Nylander skated up the ice with the puck. Matthews stayed with him the whole way. Nylander still had the puck as they made their way into the offensive zone. Then Nylander passed it to Matthews. The rookie released a quick shot, and it rocketed past the goalie. Matthews had scored four goals in his first two periods as an NHL player! No one had ever scored four goals in an NHL debut.

ALL EYES ON AUSTON

With four goals in his first NHL game, Auston Matthews caught the attention of everyone in the hockey world. Dallas Stars center Tyler Seguin wrote, "I don't even know what to say. Just a treat to watch tonight." At the rink in Arizona where Matthews grew up playing, the players stopped practice to watch Matthews. They weren't disappointed.

In the end, Matthews's amazing performance wasn't enough. Toronto lost the game 5–4 in overtime. But with an exciting young star leading the way, the future looked bright for the Maple Leafs.

DOMINANT FIRST GAME

Auston Matthews's teammate William Nylander waited until Matthews was near the goal before delivering a pass. Matthews quickly shot the puck into the net for his fourth goal of the game.

MATTHEWS
19
Svobiš
Reebok

2 STARTING IN THE SOUTHWEST

Auston Matthews was born on September 17, 1997, in San Ramon, California. He moved to Scottsdale, Arizona, when he was two years old. That's where he spent most of his childhood.

The move proved to be good timing. In 1996, the Winnipeg Jets relocated to Arizona and became the Coyotes. That meant Auston had the opportunity to attend Coyotes games as a kid. Hockey hadn't been very popular in the state

A 16-year-old Auston Matthews scores during a 2014 game against the Czech Republic.

before the Coyotes' arrival. But with an NHL team in Arizona, kids like Auston became interested in the sport.

Auston started playing hockey at five years old. He also played baseball, but hockey was always his favorite sport. Auston showed his talent from a young age. He played on a team that traveled around North America. In 2010, when Auston was 12, he played in one of the biggest youth hockey tournaments in Quebec.

More and more people began to take notice of Auston. That included USA Hockey's National Team

ICE IN THE DESERT

When the NHL came to Arizona in 1996, there were only three rinks in the entire state. But since then, the popularity of hockey has grown rapidly. From 2013 to 2018, the number of hockey players in Arizona doubled. That helped make Arizona the top state for growth in the NHL. Many hockey experts credit the Coyotes for this growth.

Matthews celebrates a goal against Canada in 2015.

Development Program. This team is based in Michigan. It selects the top young players in the United States and brings them together on one team. USA Hockey selected Auston in 2013 to be a part of the program. In two seasons with the team, Auston scored 79 goals in 104 games.

It was clear that Auston had talent. But he was too young to take part in the 2015 NHL Entry Draft. He missed the birthday cutoff by just two days. That meant he had to wait one more year before he could enter the NHL. Many players in their late teens and early twenties play in one of Canada's junior leagues. Others play college hockey in the United States. But Auston took a different route. He decided to join the ZSC Lions, a professional team in Switzerland. Auston was now competing against older, more experienced opponents. But he showed that he belonged, scoring 24 goals in 36 games.

Even though Auston was in Europe, NHL scouts still had their eyes on him. They loved

Matthews makes a move as a member of the ZSC Lions in 2015.

his quick shot. They also liked his ability to skate with the puck and keep moving without a defender taking it away. When the 2016 draft finally rolled around, most NHL scouts believed Auston was the best player available.

TORONTO
MAPLE
LEAFS
2016

3 ON THE BIG STAGE

The Toronto Maple Leafs selected Auston Matthews with the No. 1 overall pick in the 2016 draft. That made him the first American player to be selected No. 1 since Patrick Kane in 2007.

From the moment Matthews was drafted, expectations were sky high. Leafs fans hoped he could be the team's top center. They believed he could play well both offensively and defensively. Some people even compared him to the game's greats. For example, Matthews's coach in

Matthews poses in his new Maple Leafs sweater after being drafted by Toronto in 2016.

Switzerland said his release and shooting ability were similar to former NHL star Joe Sakic.

Toronto has one of the most passionate fan bases in the league. Maple Leafs players are treated like celebrities, and Matthews was no exception. Fans were asking for pictures with him before he had even played his first game. And after his four-goal debut, Matthews's popularity soared to new heights. His jersey immediately became the top seller in the NHL.

Matthews's next big moment came on January 1, 2017. Toronto faced the Detroit

A WORLD STAGE

Weeks before he started his NHL career, Matthews played for Team North America in the World Cup of Hockey. The squad was made up of top players under 23 years old. Unfortunately, the team didn't advance past the opening round. Still, Matthews and the other young players wowed fans with their skill and speed.

Matthews skates with the puck during an outdoor game against the Detroit Red Wings.

Red Wings in the NHL Centennial Classic. The Maple Leafs hosted the game at an outdoor football stadium. With the score tied 4–4 in overtime, Matthews chipped the puck over the goalie's shoulder to win the game in front of 40,000 screaming fans.

Matthews finished the 2016–17 season with an impressive 40 goals. He was the first rookie to score that many goals in more than a decade. His performance also helped Toronto make the playoffs for the first time since 2013.

The Maple Leafs faced a tough task in the first round. They were up against the Washington Capitals. The Caps had won the Presidents' Trophy, which is given to the team with the best record in the regular season.

Matthews didn't score a goal in the first two games of the series. But he redeemed himself with a goal in each of the next four games. It was a hard-fought series, with five of the games going into overtime. However, the Capitals won in Game 6.

Matthews puts one in the net against the Capitals during a 2017 playoff game.

It was a disappointing end to the season. Still, Matthews had lived up to the hype. He finished his rookie season by winning the Calder Memorial Trophy, which goes to the NHL's rookie of the year.

34
BAUER
46
34
BAUER
bauer

4 THRIVING IN TORONTO

In his second season with Toronto, Auston Matthews picked up right where he had left off. He scored 34 goals, which was second-best on the team. The Maple Leafs also made it back to the playoffs. In their first-round series against the Boston Bruins, the Leafs fell behind three games to one. However, Toronto battled back to send it to Game 7. They couldn't pull off the victory, though. Boston sent them packing with a 7–4 defeat.

Matthews looks for an open teammate during a 2018 playoff game against the Boston Bruins.

As Matthews entered the 2018–19 season, expectations were cranked up a notch when Toronto signed All-Star center John Tavares. Leafs fans expected Matthews and Tavares to deliver the team's first Stanley Cup since 1967.

Matthews got off to another hot start, scoring nine goals in five games. And in February 2019, Matthews scored the 100th goal of his career.

Toronto reached the playoffs again that season. And once again, the Leafs faced the Bruins in the first round. Matthews had a strong performance in the series, scoring five goals in all. But for the second year in a row,

PLAYING HIS HERO

As a kid, Auston Matthews had posters of Coyotes star Shane Doan on his wall. In 2016, Matthews finally got to compete against Doan. Matthews notched an assist in a 4–1 Toronto win. But Doan had an even more memorable night. He scored his 400th career goal.

Matthews snaps a powerful wrist shot against the Florida Panthers in 2019.

Boston defeated Toronto in seven games. That familiar ending was especially frustrating for Leafs fans. Even so, they hoped Matthews would continue leading Toronto to the playoffs for many years into the future.

TIMELINE

1. **San Ramon, California (September 17, 1997)**
   Auston Matthews is born.

2. **Ann Arbor, Michigan (September 13, 2013)**
   Auston plays his first game with USA Hockey's National Team Development Program.

3. **Zurich, Switzerland (August 7, 2015)**
   Auston signs a one-year contract to play with the ZSC Lions in the Swiss National League.

4. **Buffalo, New York (June 24, 2016)**
   The Toronto Maple Leafs select Matthews with the No. 1 overall pick in the 2016 NHL Entry Draft.

5. **Ottawa, Ontario (October 12, 2016)**
   Matthews makes his NHL debut for the Toronto Maple Leafs. He scores four goals in the first two periods.

6. **Washington, DC (April 13, 2017)**
   Matthews plays in his first NHL playoff game. Toronto loses to the Washington Capitals in the first round of the playoffs.

7. **Las Vegas, Nevada (February 14, 2019)**
   Matthews scores his 100th career goal in a 6–3 victory over the Vegas Golden Knights.

MAP

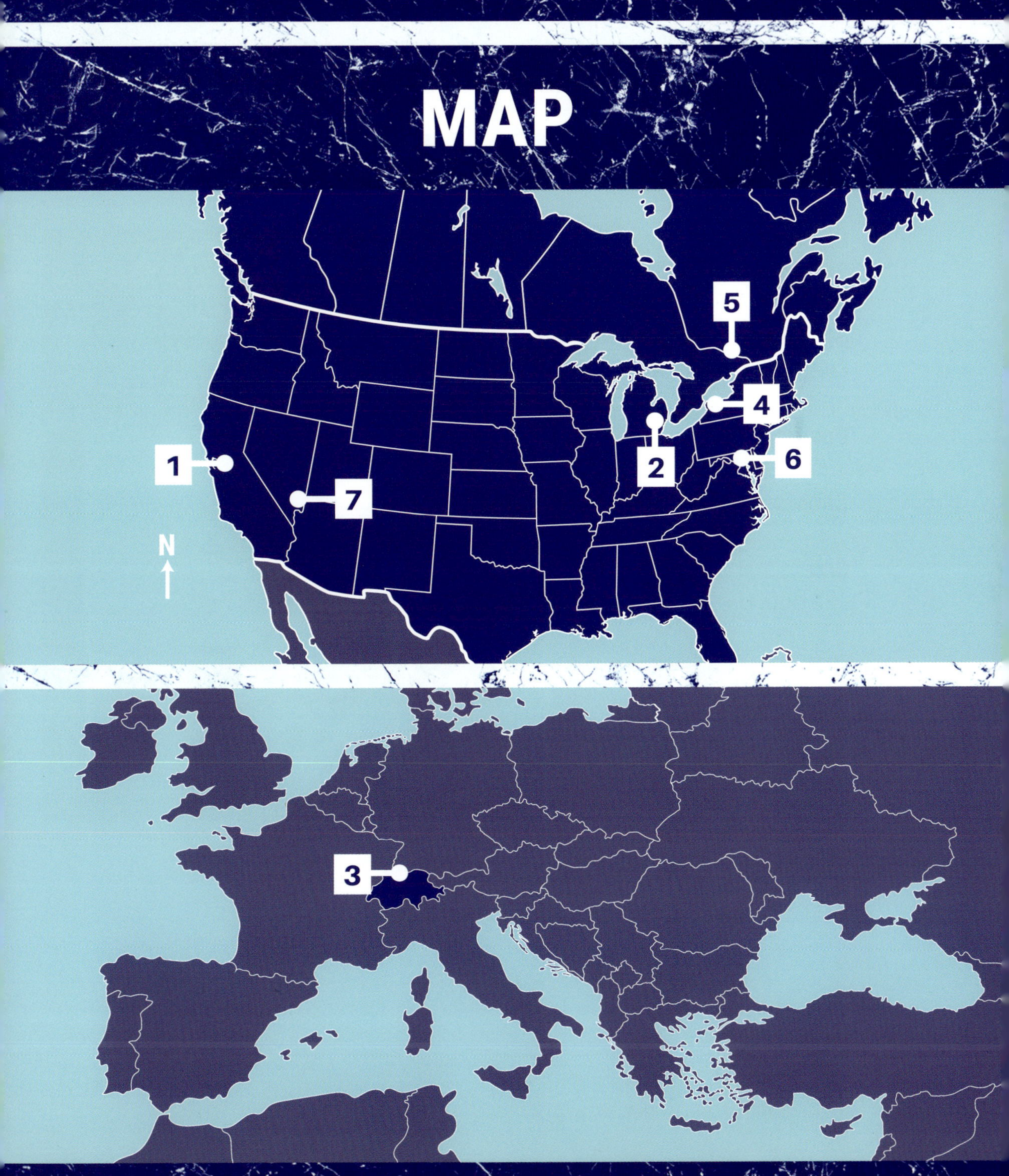

AT-A-GLANCE

Birth date:
September 17, 1997

Birthplace:
San Ramon, California

Position: Center

Shoots: Left

Size: 6 feet 3 inches, 223 pounds

NHL team: Toronto Maple Leafs (2016–)

Previous team: ZSC Lions (2015–16)

Major awards: Calder Memorial Trophy (2016–17), NHL All-Star (2017, 2018, 2019), 1st Team NHL All-Rookie Team (2016–17)

Accurate through the 2018–19 season.

GLOSSARY

assist
A pass that results in a goal.

debut
First appearance.

draft
An event that allows teams to choose new players coming into the league.

expectation
The belief that someone should achieve a goal.

hat trick
A game in which a player scores three or more goals.

one-timer
A shot that a player takes immediately after receiving a pass, without controlling the puck first.

playoffs
A set of games to decide a league's champion.

redeem
To make up for a past failure.

TO LEARN MORE

Books

Kortemeier, Todd. *Auston Matthews.* Lake Elmo, MN: Focus Readers, 2019.

Peters, Chris. *Hockey Season Ticket: The Ultimate Fan Guide.* Mendota Heights, MN: Press Box Books, 2019.

Peters, Chris. *Hockey's New Wave: The Young Superstars Taking Over the Game.* Mendota Heights, MN: Press Box Books, 2019.

Websites

Career Stats
https://www.hockey-reference.com/players/m/matthau01.html

Toronto Maple Leafs Official Site
https://www.nhl.com/mapleleafs

USA Hockey National Team Development Program
https://www.usahockeyntdp.com/

INDEX